# America's First Transcontinental Railway

*A Pictorial History of the Pacific Railroad*

by Raymond Cushing
and Jeffrey Moreau

PASADENA, CALIFORNIA

## ACKNOWLEDGMENTS

Compiling a project of this nature has brought the authors into contact with many generous and talented people. It is with a great deal of appreciation that we thank the following individuals and organizations:

For photographic contributions we have had the help of Richard Steinheimer, Shirley Burman, Dick Dorn, Clint Nestell, Kyle Wyatt, and Guy Dunscomb. Also, the Union Pacific Museum in Omaha, Nebraska, and its caretakers Don Snoddy and William Kratville; the Utah State Historical Society and its photo archivist Susan Whetstone, and the staff at the Golden Spike National Historic Site in Promontory, Utah, particularly Randy Kane.

Our wonderful map and the two hand tints of vintage photographs are the handiwork of super-talented Shirley Burman. The great front cover color illustration was executed in total color-scheme accuracy by our good friend, the noted historian and artist Kevin Bunker.

Another friend lending his historical and stylistic expertise was author and preservationist David W. Braun, who painstakingly read and offered corrections to our initial manuscript.

Raymond Cushing would like to thank librarian Jay Johnstone of the Yolo County Library in West Sacramento for his words of support.

Last but not least, Rose Loyola, mainstay of the California State Railroad Museum bookstore, offered timely encouragement when the authors first came up with the idea for this volume.

## DEDICATION

*To my mother, Julie D. Powers, for her support through the years*
*J.M.*

*To my mother and father*
*R.C.*

**Front Cover Illustration**

Central Pacific Railroad locomotive No. 62, "Whirlwind," is depicted approaching the summit of the grade leading up to the company's interchange point with the Union Pacific Railroad, Promontory, Utah with its eastbound consisting of wooden passenger cars. This scene, set shortly after noon on a breezy day in June 1869, is the creation of Sacramento artist and railroad historian Kevin Bunker.

**Back Cover Photograph**

Shortly after the driving of the legendary golden spike that marked the completion of the Pacific Railroad, photographer A.J. Russell, who was employed by the Union Pacific to record the building of the great road, posed the two locomotive engineers of the connecting companies, as well as each company's chief civil engineers, in a scene that would become famous.

**Page One Photograph**

America's greatest living railroad photographer, Richard Steinheimer, has captured the celebratory nature of the completion of the Pacific Railroad by photographing a contemporary scene at the Golden Spike National Historic Site at Promontory, Utah, where the completion scene is reenacted regularly for the numerous visitors to that historic ground.

Book Design: David M. Daly

**America's First Transcontinental Railway**


Pentrex

Published by Pentrex
P.O. Box 94911
Pasadena, CA 91109

ISBN 1-56342-002-3
Manufactured in the United States of America

First Edition: Spring 1994

# *A Pictorial History of the Pacific Railroad*

TABLE OF CONTENTS

*When most Americans think of President Abraham Lincoln, they usually associate him with the Civil War, the Gettysburg Address, and the abolition of slavery. Few remember that Lincoln's signature also authorized the biggest construction project in his time, the nation's first transcontinental railroad, linking America's East with lands in her West.*

*Up to that time, travel to and from the developed eastern states to the new territories on the other side of the continent could best be described as an ordeal. The choices were a months-long, tedious wagon train journey, or an equally long sea voyage that took one down around South America's Cape Horn. Little wonder then, that the vision of traveling to the West in a matter of just a few days excited our citizens beyond words.*

*Construction was undertaken on two fronts, from the western end of the route in Sacramento, California, and from the eastern end in Omaha, Nebraska. When at last the two segments of the new railroad were joined in 1869 with a great celebration at Promontory, Utah, a new era of American progress had begun.*

*This great project is now overshadowed by much newer and swifter transportation methods. Yet, the joining of this nation by rail remains one of the major milestones of America's evolution. Still in use today, 125 years after its completion, the original transcontinental rail route remains a major transportation corridor. It can truly be said that the early day planners and builders selected a route that has met the test of time.*

# THEODORE JUDAH...
# *and the Big Four*

*Experience had taught the young engineer that only the lure of quick profits would attract moneyed men to his plan.*

■ *Judah felt sure that a transcontinental railway was in the nation's future. "It's going to be built and I'm going to have something to do with it!"*

When Theodore Judah approached Sacramento investors in 1859 with his idea for a railroad through the Sierra Nevada mountains, he didn't describe a route that would eventually span the continent.

His previous experience—he had been laughed at by financiers in San Francisco who thought his ideas fanciful—taught him that only the lure of quick profits would attract moneyed men to his plan. So Judah told his listeners that a railroad to the silver mines of Nevada would be a bonanza for those who built and controlled it. Four shopkeepers nodded fatefully in agreement.

▲ *Mark Hopkins was the oldest of the Big Four and handled the finances of the CPRR.*

A native of Troy, New York, Judah had come to California in 1854 to build the first railway in the West—the Sacramento Valley Railroad, which ran between Sacramento and the new town of Folsom. His success in California and earlier, in Niagara Falls, New York, where he built a railway along the gorge, emboldened him to think big.

▲ *Collis P. Huntington was the chief negotiator for the Central Pacific Railroad. He spent much of his time in New York City and Washington, D.C.*

Judah, who earned the nickname "Crazy Judah" for his obsession about the Pacific Railroad, felt sure that a transcontinental railway was in the nation's future. "It's going to be built and I'm going to have something to do with it!" he told his wife, Anna.

Leaving Anna behind in Sacramento, Judah set out on horseback and sketched in notebooks a line through the foothills and the rugged Sierra, a route still generally followed by today's freight and passenger trains over Donner Pass.

Judah met with potential investors in Sacramento following his trip and made his pitch: pay for a detailed survey of a route through the Sierra, then use the survey to convince the federal government to subsidize the road. Four of his early listeners would see the plan through to fruition.

Collis P. Huntington, from Oneonta, New York, had proved to be one of Sacramento's premier traders.

◀ *Leland Stanford built a powerful political base for the Central Pacific in California, serving as governor and U.S. senator from the state. He endowed Stanford University in memory of his son, who died as a teenager.*

He would wind up as the chief negotiator for the Central Pacific Railroad.

Mark Hopkins, Huntington's partner in a hardware store, was a gaunt man who felt at home balancing books and watching expenses. He would become the railroad's money man.

Leland P. Stanford took on the responsibility of building a political base for the new railroad. He would serve as the governor of California from 1861 to 1863, and later as a U.S. Senator from the state.

Charles P. Crocker formed a construction company to build the railroad. Huntington, Hopkins and Stanford agreed to give the bulk of the contracts for building the road to Crocker's company, in which they were silent partners.

Judah laid much of the political groundwork for the new railway, successfully lobbying Congress for a Pacific Railroad Act. The 1862 bill authorized the federal government to issue bonds in the amounts of $16,000 per mile for railroad built over flat land, $32,000 for road built in the foothills, and $48,000 per mile for road built through the mountains.

The Big Four needed cash, so they argued that the foothills began just a few miles from the Sacramento city limits. They convinced both state and federal authorities of this "fact," thus entitling them to a greater subsidy early on. The idealistic Judah fought with them over this and other points, and eventually was voted out of the corporation.

The Big Four reportedly paid Judah $100,000 for his share in the Central Pacific Railroad, and agreed that he could buy out each of them for a like amount if he could raise the money. He sailed for New York to meet with investors about doing this, but he caught yellow fever while crossing Panama and died shortly after his arrival in New York in November, 1862.

When the transcontinental railroad was completed on May 10, 1869, no mention was made of Judah during the Golden Spike ceremony at Promontory, Utah.

▼ *Theodore Judah convinced four Sacramento merchants to invest in the Central Pacific Railroad. His compass is on display at the California State Railroad Museum in Sacramento.*

◀ *Charles Crocker headed the construction company that built the railroad.*

# UNION PACIFIC:

# *A Railroad is Born*

*DURANT'S MANIPULATIONS OF UNION PACIFIC STOCK WERE CONVOLUTED. BY GAINING CONTROL OF MOST OF THE RAILROAD'S STOCK, HE SEATED A COMPLIANT BOARD OF DIRECTORS.*

■ *"Oakes Ames sold stock in Credit Mobilier to his fellow members of Congress, a fact that came to light in 1872 and resulted in Ames' censure by Congress. He died a few days later."*

▲ *Thomas C. Durant served as vice-president and general manager of the Union Pacific Railroad.*

The Pacific Railroad Act of 1862 created the Union Pacific Railroad and Telegraph Company, granting the railroad odd-numbered sections of land for 10 miles either side of the right-of-way and 30 year government loan bonds as the means of financing construction of a line west from Omaha, Nebraska.

Dr. Thomas C. Durant managed to gain control of the Union Pacific in 1863 through a series of illegal stock purchases. This bold businessman gained control over the Union Pacific at the same time that Collis P. Huntington was establishing himself as the Central Pacific's lead negotiator.

Both men entered the railroad business with an eye toward making a fortune through stock manipulation. This was to remain Durant's highest goal, while Huntington would eventually embrace his role as railroad magnate.

Durant's manipulations of Union Pacific stock were convoluted. By gaining control of most of the railroad's stock, he seated a compliant board of directors that elected him vice-president and general manager, and his friend John A. Dix as president.

In 1864 Durant helped to usher a revised Pacific Railroad Act through Congress that reclassified the federal government's bonds as a second mortgage on the railroads, and allowed the Union Pacific and Central Pacific to sell their own first-mortgage bonds.

Additionally, the revised law increased the size of federal land grants, and allowed the railroads to draw on federal bonds upon the completion of each 20 miles instead of the previous 40. The two companies could also draw up to two-thirds of the bond amount due before the track was approved by federal inspectors.

A watershed development for Durant came in 1864, with formation of the Credit Mobilier of America, a holding company that ostensibly would finance construction of the Union Pacific. This company would end up owning the railroad, in violation of the Pacific Railroad Act.

Durant had two important allies in the formation of Credit Mobilier: Oakes Ames, a member of Congress, and his brother Oliver, who served as president of the railroad after Durant's eventual ouster from the board in 1867. Oakes Ames sold stock in Credit Mobilier to his fellow members of Congress, a fact that came to light in 1872 and resulted in Ames' censure by Congress in 1873. He died a few days later.

In 1864, however, these failures were in the future. With the formation of the Credit Mobilier and the adoption of the revised Pacific Railroad Act providing greater federal land grants, Thomas Durant felt he was ready to

◀ *Grenville M. Dodge was chief engineer for the Union Pacific during the time that the biggest portion of the railroad was built. A Union general in the Civil War, Dodge was widely regarded as the most capable man in the Union Pacific organization.*

▼ *Jack Casement, another former Union army general, was responsible for the track-laying construction crew. He was a fearsome boss who showed a tender side in his letters home to his wife.*

break ground for his railway.

Durant next began efforts to recruit Gen. Grenville M. Dodge as chief civil engineer for the Union Pacific. Dodge was engaged in railroad work for the Union army during the Civil War and had close ties with President Lincoln. The general eventually accepted the post when the war was over, with the provision that he have complete control in the field.

■ *"Dodge was engaged in railroad work for the Union army during the Civil War and had close ties with President Lincoln. The general eventually accepted the post when the war was over, with the provision that he have complete control in the field."*

# *Rails From The West*

*Leland Stanford shoveled a clod of dirt into a flag-draped wagon, the band played loudly, and construction of the Central Pacific Railroad was begun.*

▲ *This wooden bridge over the American River at Sacramento carried the single track of the early Central Pacific.*

■ *"Doubters tried to trip up the Big Four by spreading rumors they had no intention of building past the town of Dutch Flat, beginning of a wagon road that crossed the Sierra."*

On June 8, 1863, a crowd gathered near the levee at the foot of K Street in Sacramento to witness a historic spectacle: Gov. Leland Stanford shoveled a clod of dirt onto a flag-draped wagon, the band played loudly, and construction of the Central Pacific Railroad was begun.

Like a freight train approaching a steep grade, the new railroad required momentum to get construction underway at a rapid clip. And, as with any huge construction project, momentum meant money.

Federal subsidies would not kick in until the first 40 miles of track were laid. The Big Four would need startup money for these first 40 miles. Two sources were available: stock sales, which C.P. Huntington sought to accomplish back East, and local subsidies, which Leland Stanford as governor tried to wrangle from the state, counties and municipalities that would benefit from the railroad.

Doubters tried to trip up the Big Four by spreading rumors they had no intention of building past Dutch Flat, starting point of a wagon road controlled by the partners that crossed the Sierra. The governor and his cronies just wanted to build a road to Dutch Flat so they could monopolize trans-Sierra traffic, claimed their enemies, who dubbed the whole affair the "Dutch Flat Swindle."

One way the Big Four improved their initial financial position was by convincing the federal government that the Sierra foothills began at Arcade Creek, just seven miles from downtown Sacramento. This distinction entitled them to $32,000 per mile in government bonds, instead of the $16,000 to which they were entitled for building along the flat valley floor.

With Charles Crocker in the field constructing the railroad by trial and error, the Central Pacific reached Junction (later Roseville) by the end of 1863. The next goal was Newcastle, 12 miles farther east.

◀ *The trestle at Newcastle was the CPRR's first major structural undertaking.*

▲ *A steam locomotive changes direction atop the turntable at Rocklin, California.*

Charles Crocker hired subcontractors for the run to Newcastle. The subcontractors managed only to build two miles of track, however, and Crocker and his crews were forced to complete the work to Newcastle. Here the first outcroppings of granite could be found, a harbinger of the difficult years that would be spent crossing the Sierra Nevada with the road.

By the time the 31 miles to Newcastle had been completed, the Big Four were borrowing money on their own personal credit to pay for the construction work. Public confidence in the railroad reached its lowest ebb around this time. All four of the principals heard dire warnings from friends, concerned that they would lose their personal fortunes trying to cross the Sierra with a railroad.

■ *"On July 2, 1864, President Linoln signed the revised Pacific Railway Act, doubling the amount of land grants and making the government bonds a second mortgage on the railroad."*

The Big Four were not completely disheartened as they approached the Herculean task of crossing the Sierra. On July 2, 1864, President Linoln signed the revised Pacific Railroad Act, doubling the amount of land grants and making the government bonds a second mortgage on the railroad.

The Big Four were gambling that the risks they were taking would translate into huge profits down the road.

◀ *Central Pacific locomotive No. 2, "Pacific," crosses the Little Truckee River with a trainload of cross-ties in 1867.*

▲ *A CPRR construction train passes through Bloomer Cut in the Sierra foothills in 1867. This hand-dug wonder is 65 feet deep and 800 feet long.*

# Conquering the Sierra

ADD TO THE GRANITE TERRAIN WINTER TEMPERATURES THAT DIPPED BELOW ZERO AND SNOW BANKS THAT REACHED THIRTY FEET OR MORE, AND THE ACHIEVEMENTS OF THE CENTRAL PACIFIC CONSTRUCTION CREWS BECOME EVEN MORE IMPRESSIVE.

■ *"The Asians outworked their European co-workers. They almost never drank whiskey. They bathed daily and they experienced few absences from work due to illness."*

▲ *Workers pause with their wagons at Heath Ravine, 82 miles east of Sacramento. This mammoth grading project was typical of the jobs undertaken by the CPRR's Chinese construction crews.*

Mainly on the strength of its crossing the Sierra Nevada mountain range, the Central Pacific Railroad was destined to become known for its engineering and construction feats.

Under the terms of the Pacific Railroad Act, the Central Pacific was issued bonds in the amount of $48,000 per mile of track laid through the mountains. The railroad worked hard to earn this money, clearing a roadbed through a solid granite landscape where the progress was often measured in inches per day. Add to the granite terrain winter temperatures that dipped below zero and snow banks that reached 30 feet or more, and the achievements of the Central Pacific construction crews—working without power tools—become even more impressive.

Orchestrating the Central Pacific's drive through the Sierra were construction boss Charles Crocker and his foreman James H. Strobridge. To Chinese laborers fell the responsibility of building the Sierra route, almost by default.

By 1865 the labor shortage on the Central Pacific had become critical, as miners-turned-railroad workers would abandon the line each time there was word of a new ore strike. Crocker was the first to suggest employing Chinese workers. Strobridge's response was, "I will not boss Chinese!"

Prejudice against Chinese immigrants ran high in California; in 1858 the legislature even outlawed Chinese immigration, but the ban was not enforced. Crocker met Strobridge's resistance with the observation that the Chinese had two relevant achievements to their credit: they had invented gunpowder and they had built the Great Wall. Fifty Chinese workers were hired on a trial basis.

The Asians outworked their European co-workers. They almost never drank whiskey. They bathed daily and they experienced few absences from work due to illness. The Chinese workers earned the admiration of their new bosses and at one point Crocker had 10,000 Chinese workers on his line at the same time.

At the time that the Central Pacific crews were bridging the Sierra, making only inches a day, the Union Pacific crews were crossing the plains at the rate of a mile per day. The Big Four may have felt frustrated by their comparatively slow pace, but they didn't become discouraged. While Charles Crocker acted as field marshal for his construction army, Collis P. Huntington continued to buy rolling stock and material for the rail-

◀ *A full-size locomotive that was hauled around the mountain while Summit Tunnel was under construction is shown on the isolated section of track along the Truckee River.*

road in the East.

By August, 1865, the end of track was at the village of Illinoistown, which was renamed for Speaker of the House Schuyler Colfax of Indiana when he paid a visit. The winter of 1865-66 was relatively mild compared to the following winter, when some 40 feet of snow fell and Chinese workers spent the season living in sheds under the snow drifts. Their days or nights (there were 'round-the-clock shifts in the winter of 1866-67) were spent chipping and blasting in the tunnels.

Avalanches, blasting accidents and frostbite were a few of the ways in which Central Pacific workers in the Sierra died. Some workers just wandered off into the snow and were never seen again.

Unfortunately, incomplete records were kept, so the exact number of those who gave their lives in the battle for the Sierra will probably never be known.

▲ *Above, the 1,659-foot long Summit Tunnel, constructed at an elevation of 7,042 feet, is shown prior to completion. At left, CPRR Locomotive No. 13, "Hercules," hauls a load of hay through Cisco, California in 1868, when the line was open as far as Truckee.*

◀ *Workmen prepare to haul fill from Owl Gap Cut, a 900-foot-long and 45-foot-deep cut through the Sierra that was another of the huge excavation jobs characteristic of those undertaken by the Chinese workers.*

# *Starting from the East*

*THE LOGISTICS OF SUPPLYING THE RAILHEAD AT OMAHA WERE ASTOUNDING. THE NEAREST RAIL SERVICE WAS OVER 100 MILES EAST NEAR GRINNELL, IOWA, OR 175 MILES DOWNSTREAM WHERE THE HANNIBAL & ST. JOSEPH RAILROAD MET THE MISSOURI RIVER.*

■ *"He was able to do this because when he agreed to become chief engineer he insisted that he have complete command over the construction crews."*

Ground was broken for the Union Pacific line on December 2, 1863, but it would be 18 months before the first rail was laid.

Much of the delay would be directly attributable to the curious management style of Thomas Durant, who insisted on making even small decisions himself. He was even known to foment discontent among conflicting interests, just to gain more time to make up his own mind!

Durant had stirred up quite a debate in Omaha, the eastern terminus of the railroad, when he approved stretching the line in an ox-bow to add nine miles to the route (and considerable additional revenue to his coffers). He also had dangled the possibility of moving the terminus up or down the Missouri River.

The logistics of supplying the railhead at Omaha were astounding. The nearest rail service was over 100 miles east near Grinnell, Iowa, or 175 miles downstream where the Hannibal & St. Joseph Railroad met the Missouri River. Most of the year the Missouri was not navigable by steamboat, which meant that all the supplies for the building of the railroad would have to be carted by wagon across Iowa to the Missouri.

The Pacific Railroad Act required completion of the first 100 miles by June 27, 1866. When the first rail was laid on July 10, 1865, the Union Pacific, which had failed to build a single mile of track in 18

▲ *Union Pacific locomotive No. 23 at Wyoming Station, situated 15 miles west of Laramie. At right, a load test of the Union Pacific's Devil's Gate bridge with three locomotives and two caboose cars.*

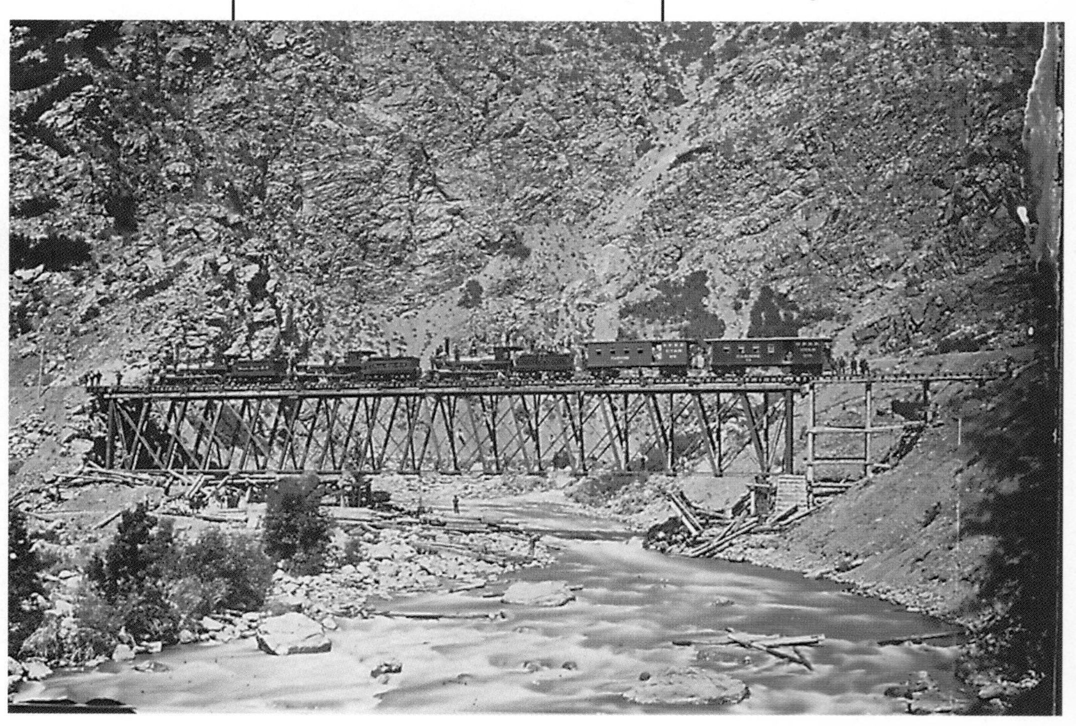

▼ *Looking east at Green River, Wyoming, with Citadel Rock at left. The train at right is on a temporary trestle with workers at left constructing granite piers for the permanent bridge.*

months, would now have to build 100 miles of line in its first year of actual construction.

Durant's strength, as it turned out, was in choosing the principal figures for his construction operation. Grenville Dodge, freed of his Civil War military obligations, was appointed chief engineer, a post he was not able to fill until May, 1866, following an Indian affairs conference.

John S. "Jack" Casement became the chief tracklayer. He was only five feet four, but had made a name for himself as a gallant soldier in the Civil War, attaining the rank of brigadier general.

Dodge provided the leadership that had been sorely lacking in the Union Pacific organization. He was able to do this because when he agreed to become chief engineer he insisted that he have complete command over the construction crews.

Dodge would report to Durant in New York, but everyone in the field would report to Dodge. This would eliminate the untenable situation that had existed in which the heads of various branches of the organization had all reported to Durant.

The military influence that Dodge and Casement brought to the construction operation resulted in the required 100 miles being built by June 4, and 247 miles completed by October 6, 1866, when the railroad reached the 100th meridian. Durant seized this occasion as an opportunity for a big party. Dignitaries, government commissioners, reporters, Union Pacific directors, senators, congressmen, and financiers all traveled to the 100th meridian in new Pullman Palace sleeping cars, compliments of the Union Pacific.

▼ *U.P. locomotive No. 120 and train crossing Weber River in Utah, with tunnel No. 3 to the rear of the train.*

■ *"Once the party reached the railhead, they dined on game and champagne, watched the crew lay track, and saw a mock battle and war dance performed by Shawnee warriors."*

Once the party reached the railhead, they dined on game and champagne, watched the crew lay track, and saw a mock battle and war dance performed by Shawnee warriors.

# *Hell On Wheels*

*"Restaurant and saloon keepers, gamblers, desperadoes of every grade, the vilest of men and women made up this 'Hell on Wheels,' as it was most aptly termed."*

■ *"An enduring legend has it that only Irish worked on the Union Pacific construction crews, but this isn't true."*

The makeshift towns that sprang up along the route of the Union Pacific as it was being built became widely known as "Hell on Wheels," after a Massachusetts newspaper man toured the road and filed a report from the end of track.

"Restaurant and saloon keepers, gamblers, desperadoes of every grade, the vilest of men and women made up this 'Hell on Wheels,' as it was most aptly termed," wrote Samuel Bowles, editor of the *Springfield Republican.*

Julesburg, Colorado, Benton, Wyoming, and Corinne, Utah, were originally Hell on Wheels. Other communities—Laramie and Cheyenne among them—started life as Hell on Wheels towns and evolved into vibrant cities, complete with schools and churches. The temporary oases of whiskey, gambling and prostitution stretched from Kearney, Nebraska, to Corinne, picking up and following the end of track whenever it moved, like a tired hound dog trailing its master.

▲ *With desolate vistas such as this, it is easy to understand how Union Pacific workers were lured to the distractions of the "Hell on Wheels" establishments.*

The tracklayers were drunk much of the time they were in town. Together with prostitutes, pimps, and gamblers (some of whom wouldn't think twice about killing a man), they created a nest of mayhem and depravity.

An enduring legend has it that only Irish worked on the Union Pacific construction crews, but this isn't true. Scots, Mexicans, and Civil War veterans of varied European descent, from both the North and the South, mingled with Blacks and Scandinavians on the work crews. The only criteria that the Casement brothers had for their workers were that they be strong, and willing to tackle the job assigned them with military gusto.

In post-Civil War America there was no shortage of men with these qualifications who needed work. There was also no shortage of opportunists who saw the Union Pacific crew of 1,000 thirsty and lonely men as a ready market for liquor, sex, and gambling. A Hell on Wheels town could spring to life in as little as a month. Julesburg reportedly swelled in population from 41 in June, 1863, to 4,000 in July.

Occasionally Jack Casement

would range through these rowdy settlements, restoring a semblance of order by firing a few well-aimed shots. This was the case in Julesburg, when General Dodge received word that gamblers were seizing lots being sold by the railroad without paying for them.

Dodge ordered Casement to get the situation under control. Accompanied by two hundred men, "General Jack" entered the town at night and conferred with the recalcitrant gamblers. When no agreement could be reached, Casement ordered his men to fire at will. A few gamblers wound up in the cemetery and the rest agreed to pay for their lots forthwith.

Alcohol continued to be a problem throughout the building of the transcontinental line for the Union Pacific bosses. Unlike the Central Pacific's Chinese workers, the Europeans and Americans who made up the bulk of the Union Pacific crew had a voracious taste for spirits. On at least one occasion the railroad supervisors took matters into their own hands and destroyed a half-dozen "whiskey ranches," as the makeshift saloons that followed the end of track were called.

■ *"Unlike the Central Pacific's Chinese workers, the Europeans and Americans who made up the bulk of the Union Pacific crew had a voracious taste for spirits."*

▲ *Bear River, 965 miles west of Omaha, epitomized the "Hell-on-Wheels" towns that sprang up along the Union Pacific route. When this photo was taken the town reportedly had a population of 200, which dwindled to zero when the end-of-track moved farther west.*

# THE CENTRAL PACIFIC: *Early Service*

CHARLES CROCKER'S TRACKLAYERS HAD COMPLETED 18 MILES OF TRACK IN THE FOUR MONTHS SINCE THE FIRST SPIKE WAS DRIVEN IN SACRAMENTO.

■ *"The train broke down for a while inside the Summit Tunnel, scaring the wits out of the legislators and dignitaries aboard, who gasped for breath in the smoke-filled darkness until the train could be restarted."*

▲ *An excursion train using borrowed Sacramento Valley Railroad passenger cars stops at Cisco station in the Sierra Nevada mountains. Cisco (inset) was a busy stop along the CPRR tracks during the railway's construction.*

The Central Pacific crews reached Junction (Roseville) on February 19, 1864. Charles Crocker's tracklayers had completed 18 miles of track in the four months since the first spike was driven in Sacramento.

On April 25 the new railroad announced regular passenger service to Junction. In the first week 298 passengers bought tickets to ride on the three trains running daily in each direction, and earnings were $354.25.

By early June the tracks were 31 miles out, at Newcastle, and regular passenger and freight service to that town commenced on June 6. The trains ran between the terminals at about 20 miles per hour.

In the next year and a half the railroad gained only 20 more miles of finished track, due primarily to a slowdown in the availability of cash. Also, the construction crews were facing for the first time the granite outcroppings of the Sierra. The first big hurdle was Bloomer Cut, which consumed so much blasting powder in its 800 foot length that it outstripped the Central Pacific's ability to keep pace with expenses.

The tracks reached Dutch Flat by the summer of 1866, connecting there with the Big Four's own wagon road over the Sierra. This resulted in a much needed boost to the railroad's revenues, enabling the four partners to replenish their depleted fortunes. The tracks reached Cisco, 92 miles out, in November, when work was halted by heavy snow.

In addition to commercial service, the Big Four hosted a series of promotional excursions to keep legislators, politicians, and the public informed of their progress. These outings usually went well, but Leland Stanford did more damage than good by organizing an excursion into the Sierra in December, 1868.

The train broke down for a while inside the Summit Tunnel, scaring the wits out of the legislators and dignitaries aboard, who gasped for breath in the smoke-filled darkness until the train could be restarted. The excursion was also ill-fated in that sparks caused a couple of the luxurious cars brought out for the occasion to catch fire! The ride itself was generally uncomfortable, although prior to the mishaps the excursionists had marveled at the dramatic mountain views.

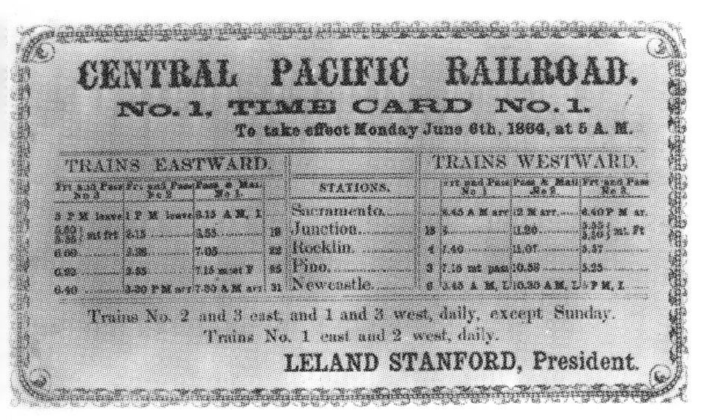

# CENTRAL PACIFIC RAILROAD.

## No. 1, TIME CARD No. 1.

To take effect Monday June 6th, 1864, at 5 A. M.

| TRAINS EASTWARD. | | | | | | TRAINS WESTWARD. | | |
|---|---|---|---|---|---|---|---|---|
| Fr't and Pass No 3 | Fr't and Pass No 2 | Pass & Mail No 1 | | STATIONS. | | Fr't and Pass No 1 | Pass & Mail No 2 | Fr't and Pass No 3 |
| 5 P M leave | 1 P M leave | 3.15 A M, 1 | | Sacramento | | 8.45 A M arr | 12 M arr | 6.40 P M ar |
| 5.50 / 5.55 mt frt | 2.15 | 3.55 | 18 | Junction | 18 | 8 | 11.20 | 5.55 / 5.20 mt. Ft |
| 6.00 | 2.28 | 7.05 | 22 | Rocklin | 4 | 7.40 | 11.07 | 5.37 |
| 6.20 | 2.55 | 7.15 mt F | 25 | Pino | 3 | 7.15 mt pass | 10.50 | 5.25 |
| 6.40 | 3.20 P M arr | 7.30 A M arr | 31 | Newcastle | 6 | 6.45 A M, L | 10.30 A M, L | 5 P M, L |

Trains No. 2 and 3 east, and 1 and 3 west, daily, except Sunday.
Trains No. 1 east and 2 west, daily.

LELAND STANFORD, President.

◀ *The first timetable issued by the Central Pacific Railroad shows service available to Newcastle, in the Sierra foothills, as of June 6, 1864.*

▶ *A train travels through Hog's Back Cut with an eastbound manifest in the early years of Central Pacific service. Writers and journalists recorded the impressive vistas for their readers back East.*

▲ *An early Central Pacific passenger train negotiates a grade at Bear Valley en route to Cisco.*

▼ *A nine-car excursion train passes by a group of horsemen just below Dutch Flat in the Sierra foothills.*

▲ *A CPRR locomotive winds its way along the track above the American River Canyon 71 miles east of Sacramento.*

# Battling the Snow

San Francisco financiers shook their heads back in the 1850s when "Crazy Judah" talked about building a railroad through the Sierra.

■ *"At one point during the winter of 1867 the Central Pacific crews mimicked Hannibal crossing the Alps."*

San Francisco financiers shook their heads back in the 1850s when "Crazy Judah" talked about building a railroad through the Sierra. The capitalists saw two major obstacles to building through the mountains: the granite and the snow.

Central Pacific crews ran into relatively mild winters in 1864-65 and 1865-66. But the winter of 1866-67 was destined to go down in history as one of the worst in the Sierra, with 40 feet of snow falling.

The Chinese workers were not used to the brutal winter conditions and untold numbers of them died of frostbite. Some of them reportedly became disoriented and wandered off into the wilderness, never to be seen again.

Avalanches also took their toll, although the exact number of victims is not known. Those buried in avalanches were often by necessity left until the spring thaw, when their bodies could be found and shipped back to China for burial. The massive snow slides were often brought on by blasting that was being done for the tunnels being driven through the Sierra.

During the winter the workers lived in sheds under the snow drifts, and dug tunnels to make their way to and from their sheds to the work site—usually a tunnel inside the giant mountains. It was said that scores of the workers toiled all winter without ever seeing the sun.

Aside from the human cost of the epic winter of 1866-67, the severe conditions made apparent the need for some method of protecting the tracks from drifting snow in order to keep service running consistently. Crews frequently would have to clear the track by hand, with shovels. Various designs of snow plows were also tried during this period, in an effort to keep the supply trains moving to the railhead.

▲ *A snow shed winds past the station at Summit, California. A crew of 2,500 men worked full-time on building the sheds in 1868.*

◀ *Rotary plows like the one shown at left cleared the tracks in later years.*

◀ *At left, a bucker-type snow plow makes its way along the Central Pacific main line in the Sierra Nevada in 1887. Above, a steam locomotive leaves the covered turntable under the snow shed at Summit, California. At top, the entrance to a Sierra tunnel was protected by this primitive snow shed.*

Snowsheds became a permanent solution to the problem on some of the most vulnerable stretches of track. These were massive wooden structures with walls bolted to the granite cliffs, built from posts the size of utility poles and covered with roof planks up to five inches thick.

In the years 1868 and 1869 the Central Pacific built nearly 38 miles of snowsheds, costing approximately $2 million. Not only did the heavy materials keep the price of building the sheds high, but the skilled carpenters who were needed to build them commanded high pay in California at that time.

At one point during the winter of 1867 the Central Pacific crews mimicked Hannibal crossing the Alps. The weather in the High Sierra caused a halt to track-laying and the Summit Tunnel was not completed yet, so the decision was made to send crews ahead to the Truckee River Canyon, where the weather was milder.

Tracklaying equipment needed to be transported along the graded right-of-way and around unfinished tunnels and bridges on special sleds. In all, the crews conveyed an incredible array of equipment: 16,000 rails, 40 freight and platform cars and three standard-size locomotives!

*The sign that marked the CPRR's success in building ten miles of track in one day.*

# *The Ten Mile Day*

THE MOTIVE, AS ALWAYS, WAS MONEY. THE RAILROAD THAT LAID DOWN THE MOST MILES OF TRACK WOULD RECEIVE THE GREATEST AMOUNT IN FEDERAL BONDS.

*"President Ulysses Grant put a stop to the speculation by ordering Congress to select a site. Congress approved the choice and the race was over."*

*Looking east from the railhead at Iron Point, Nevada, this view shows the vast wilderness that faced the CPRR crews after they descended the Sierra.*

The revised Pacific Railroad Act of 1864 stated that the Central Pacific could build up to 150 miles beyond the California line.

C.P. Huntington was determined to have that provision altered to allow the railroad building from the west to build as far as it could until it met the Union Pacific building from the east. The motive, as always, was money. The railroad that laid down the most miles of track would receive the greatest amount in federal bonds.

In June, 1866, Huntington's lobbying paid off. Congress passed bills that effectively turned the building of the transcontinental line into a great race. The Central Pacific could build as far and as fast as it could until it met the Union Pacific railhead.

At the time Congress made its decision, the Central Pacific was still struggling through the Sierra. Blasting and building as fast as they could, the crews often made very little progress.

The CP's opportunity to "make tracks" came when it began building in Nevada in 1868. The construction workers received bonuses to compensate for their occasionally collapsing in the heat and experiencing dehydration. Meanwhile, foreman Strobridge experienced regular one-mile (of tracklaying) days and even his first two-mile days.

It wasn't until June 18, 1868, that the first train to cross the Sierra chugged into the new settlement of Reno. Even though the CP had been building in the Nevada desert, the incomplete Summit Tunnel kept the line from being a continuous one. Making the line contiguous fulfilled the requirements of the Pacific Railroad Act and freed up $10 million in goverment bonds, welcome relief for the cash-starved railroad.

Congress wisely reserved the right to select a site where the railroads would join. By the early part of 1869, the grading and roadbed crews of the two companies were duplicating each other's work. For miles in the Utah desert, the two crews worked parallel to each other, both unsure which railroad would manage to get track laid first.

President Ulysses Grant put a stop to the speculation by ordering Congress to select a site. The decision to join the railroads at Promontory, Utah, was actually made by General Dodge and C.P. Huntington, who met at the Washington home of Congressman Samuel Hooper in an all-night session that stretched well into the next day. Congress approved the choice and the race was over.

An important part of the contest hadn't been settled, however. Early on, Thomas Durant had bet Charles Crocker that the Central

◄ *A Central Pacific construction train, headed by locomotive No. 27, "Goliah," passes through Wadsworth, Nevada.*

Pacific crews could not live up to Crocker's boast that they could build 10 miles of track in one day. Crocker set April 28, 1869, as the day that his crew of several hundred workmen could lay 10 miles of track across the flat Utah desert. The rest of the workmen of both companies were given a holiday.

The Central Pacific crew succeeded in laying the 10 miles of track and a sign attesting to the fact was erected at the site. In all, the workers had driven the spikes for 3,520 rails into 25,800 ties to achieve the 10 mile mark.

◄ *At left is the CPRR construction superintendent's car at the end of track. Below, construction chief J.H. Strobridge poses in his suit atop a flat car at the construction camp at Victory, Utah, on May 1, 1869.*

▲ *At top, a work train and crew train sit waiting amid the hills of Nevada to be moved to the east when more line is completed. Above, a CPRR construction train at Sentinel Rock, 20 miles west of Carlin, Nevada.*

# THE LAST LEG:

# *Crossing Zion*

*In the 20 years that the Mormons had been in Utah, they had experienced prosperity as a by-product of their trade with placer miners ...and the boom that accompanied the Civil War.*

■ *"Arrangements were made for the pilgrims to travel free on the Union Pacific from Omaha to the railhead in Utah."*

The Latter-Day Saints, or Mormons, of Utah were to play an important part in the completion of the last legs of the transcontinental railroad. The Mormons viewed the coming of the railroad as a blessing for two reasons. It would provide a means of transporting their agricultural products to lucrative markets, and it would provide construction jobs for their young men.

In the 20 years that the Mormons had been in Utah, they had experienced prosperity as a by-product of their trade with placer miners in Montana and as part of the general commercial boom that accompanied the Civil War. By 1865, however, the war was over, mining had ebbed, and the Mormons were experiencing tighter economic times.

In 1868 Thomas Durant wired Mormon leader Brigham Young, asking if he would be willing to enter into a contract to provide roadbed grading from Echo Canyon toward Salt Lake. He asked the Mormon leader to name his price and within two weeks Young had signed a contract with the Union Pacific. (The Mormons subsequently agreed to help grade the CPRR roadbed, as well.)

Brigham Young believed the opportunity was a godsend, offering a chance for his people to escape the onus of debt that had begun to accumulate. Young's only concern was that the railroad might require so many young men that it

▸ *The Mormons lobbied to have the transcontinental railway pass through Salt Lake City, but had to settle for building the Utah Central to connect the Mormon capital with the mainline at Ogden, Utah.*

◀ *Brigham Young, patriarch of the Latter Day Saints in Utah Territory, embraced the transcontintal railway as a means of assuring the economic future of his Mormon followers.*

would jeopardize the Mormons' work in the fields.

To head off such a situation, he sent out a call to Liverpool, England, for more Mormon pilgrims to set out on their annual migration earlier in the year than usual. Arrangements were made for the pilgrims to travel free on the Union Pacific from Omaha to the railhead in Utah.

Heading up the Mormon work crews were Young's three sons, Brigham Young, Jr., John W. Young, and Joseph A. Young, along with Bishop John Sharp. Newspapers in neighboring Wyoming accused Brigham Young of profiteering in the enterprise, citing the requirement that every Mormon ward provide manpower for the project and the deduction from each worker's pay of a 10 percent tithe to the church.

The chronically cash-strapped Union Pacific made things difficult for the Mormon managers, more so than it might have appeared to outsiders. Young was required to advance as much as $50,000 of his own funds to keep the work crews at their posts when railroad funds were late.

Brigham Young lobbied heavily for the railroad to pass through Salt Lake on its way westward, but to no avail. He wound up settling some of the Union Pacific's debts in exchange for railroad equipment to set up the Utah Central, a line that connected the Mormon capital with the main transcontinental line at Ogden.

# *The Road that Linked*

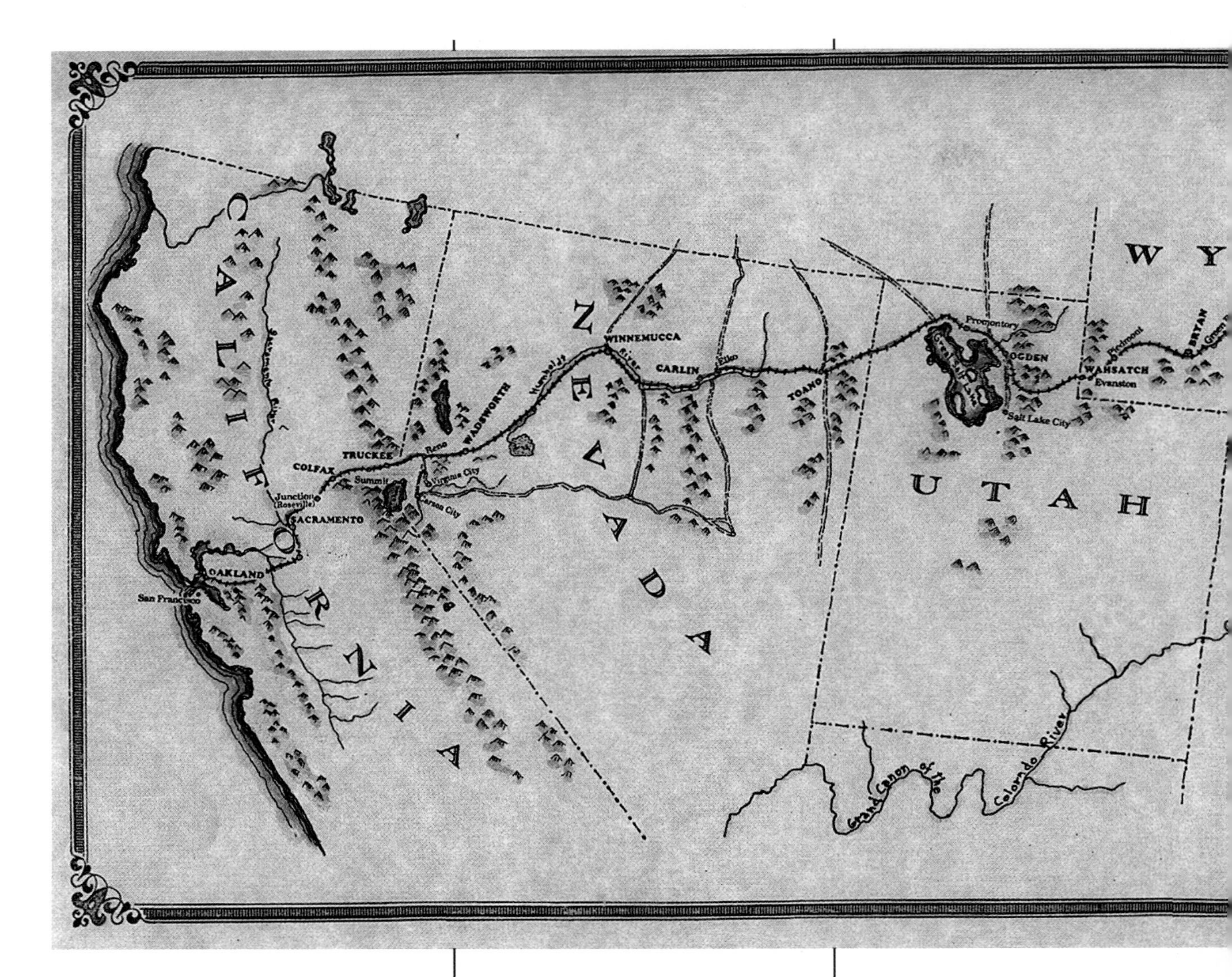


*This letter, dated May 1944, was addressed to A. T. Mercier, president of Southern Pacific Company, San Francisco.*

## An Early Rider Reminisces

*Dear Sir:*

*The recent celebration of the 75th anniversary of driving the "Golden Spike" in the month of May 1869 (completing the link between the East and West by rail) brought to my mind the thrill I had as a boy of nine years when I made the trip from York, Pa. to San Francisco in December, 1869.*

*Some of the things I remember will never again be seen by human eyes: my first glimpse of the vast herds of buffalo being hunted by bands of Indians across the Plains, and I can still see the old coaches with open platforms and connected by a single link coupling. The old "smoky" oil lamps, and the little cannon style coal stoves at each end of the coach.*

*And in winter, you did not have much choice of seats as to comfort, for if you drew a seat near the stove you would roast, and in the center you would freeze. I remember how the Indians would pile on the "blind baggage" to ride the "wagon" pulled by*

# a Nation

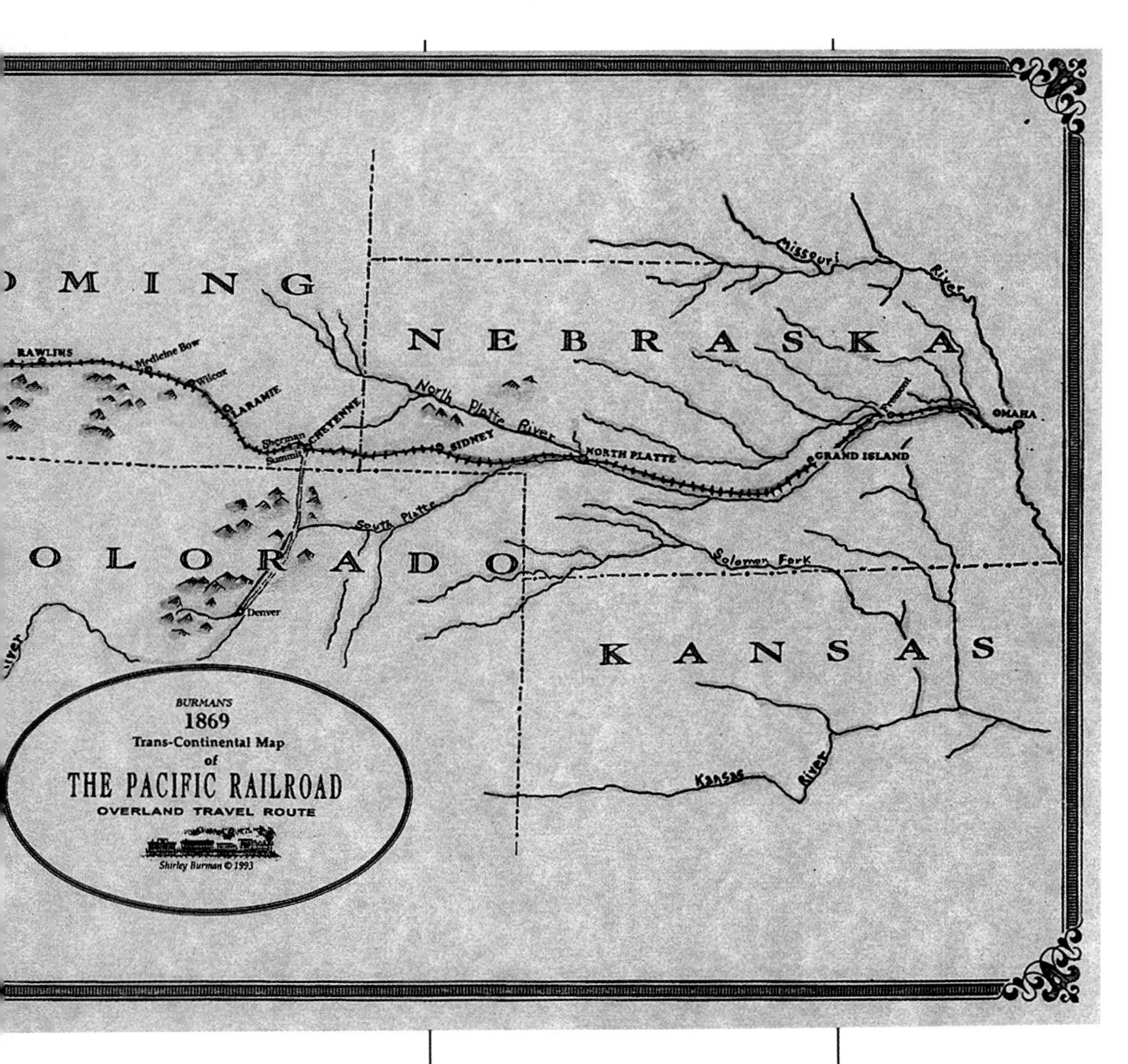


*◀What had been virtually two countries divided by a great desert became one with the completion of the Pacific Railroad. Interstate 80 today closely follows the route of the original transcontinental railway.*

*the "iron horse."*

*It was also a thrill when I had my first glimpse of a sailing ship in San Francisco Bay, for I had never seen a ship, only in books. It was a beautiful moonlit night, and I saw those ships and decided I would see them more closely. The following morning I was missing from the hotel. When found by the police, I was lying on a pile of sacks taking in the sights no one will again see.*

*Each time I have occasion to travel your lines, I cannot help but marvel at the change in equipment from that of 1869. The old wood coach of that date is the "streamliner" of today with air-conditioned coaches and all the comforts a traveler could wish for. During pre-war times it was a real joy to travel and even now at the age of 84 I still like to ride the "streamliner."*

*I hope you will pardon me for writing to you, as I know you have more important business to occupy your time, but I wanted you to know there are still a few living who made that journey 75 years ago.*

*Yours truly,*

*William P. Schlosser*
*Los Angeles*

# ALONG THE ROUTE:

# *Ready Made Cities*

*WHEN CONSTRUCTION OF THE TRANSCONTINENTAL RAILWAY STARTED IN 1863 THERE WERE NO CITIES BETWEEN OMAHA AND SACRAMENTO, EXCEPT SALT LAKE CITY IN THE TERRITORY OCCUPIED BY THE LATTER-DAY SAINTS.*

■ *"Cheyenne was named by General Dodge in grudging admiration for the Indian warriors who threatened the early construction of the railroad."*

When construction of the transcontinental railway started in 1863 there were no cities between Omaha and Sacramento, except Salt Lake City in the territory occupied by the Latter-Day Saints.

While most of the Hell on Wheels towns dried up and disappeared after the Union Pacific's end-of-track moved on, some of the railroad settlements on the Plains became full-fledged cities.

In Nebraska, Grand Island, North Platte, and Sidney grew into communities with churches, schools and city governments. Omaha, too, derived its identity from the existence of the railroad, and grew into a metropolis of the Midwest.

In Wyoming, Laramie, Rawlins, and Cheyenne grew up alongside the tracks into vibrant cities. Cheyenne was named by General Dodge in grudging admiration for the Indian warriors who threatened the early construction of the railroad.

The Central Pacific founded its own share of towns, although the free-drinking, whoring, and gambling of the Hell on Wheels towns never took hold in the ranks of the CP's Chinese workers. They were content with their daily intake of the opium that many of them carried in a leather bag.

▶ *Before construction of the transcontinental railway, Salt Lake was already a pristine community. The coming of the railroads assured its future as an important American city.*

◀ *The second railroad station in Reno, Nevada, opened in June 1868. This combination hotel, restaurant and depot burned to the ground on May 25, 1886, in a fire that destroyed most of the business section of Reno. Because early trains carried no dining cars, stops had to made to allow passengers the opportunity to refresh themselves.*

■ *"The City of Reno was named for General Jesse L. Reno, a well known Civil War figure. In California, Truckee and Colfax were communities that grew up around the railroad yards and still thrive."*

◀ *Once the transcontinental railroad was up and running, Sacramento warmed to its arrival by building this elegant arcade-type station.*

▼ *Cheyenne, Wyoming, came into existence as a result of the building of the transcontinental railway. This view down 16th Street shows the plains starting at the edge of town.*

In Nevada, the Central Pacific gave birth to the towns of Elko, Winnemucca, and Humboldt Wells (now Wells). The City of Reno was founded by the Central Pacific and named for General Jesse L. Reno, a well known Civil War figure. In California, Truckee and Colfax were communities that grew up around the railroad yards and still thrive.

# THE TRANSCONTINENTAL: *Dawn of Service*

> *Plans for the ceremony marking the completion of the Pacific Railroad were not even formalized until the morning of May 10.*

> ■ *"Following the speeches, Stanford and Durant took turns gently tapping the precious metal spikes into the ceremonial tie."*

For all its durability as a legend, the Golden Spike ceremony that took place on May 10, 1869 at Promontory Summit, Utah was surprisingly impromptu. Plans for the ceremony marking the completion of the Pacific Railroad were not even formalized until the morning of May 10. Reporters had been told the event would take place on May 8, but Union Pacific officials didn't arrive in time, delayed by bad weather and irate workmen who hadn't been paid.

The key ingredients in the pageant were a laurelwood tie (the "last tie"), ceremonial spikes donated by the states of Nevada and Arizona; a smaller gold spike donated by the San Francisco *News-Letter*, and the Golden Spike itself. The famous spike had been ordered by a friend of Leland Stanford's as a fitting commemorative. The 17.6 carat spike was nearly six inches long and contained $350 in gold.

Emcee for the ceremony was Sacramento banker Edgar Mills, who introduced H.W. Harkness, a Sacramento newspaper publisher and editor, who in turn presented two ceremonial spikes to Leland Stanford (including the Golden Spike) and two to Union Pacific Vice-President Thomas Durant. Stanford delivered a spirited address, but Durant demurred, claiming a headache (possibly brought on by drinking at a party the night before in Ogden). In Durant's place, Union Pacific engineer Grenville Dodge delivered a few enthusiastic words.

Following the speeches, Stanford and Durant took turns gently tapping the precious metal spikes into the ceremonial tie. The laurelwood tie and the commemorative spikes were immediately removed and replaced with a pine tie, into which three ordinary iron spikes were driven. A fourth spike was wired to the transcontinental telegraph line so the entire country could "hear" the final spike being driven.

Stanford took a swing at the final spike and hit the tie instead. Durant tried, but unsteadily missed hitting even the tie! A regular railroad worker then stepped up and drove the spike home, and a telegrapher sent the fateful message, "D-O-N-E" across the country, at 12:47 p.m., Monday, May 10, 1869.

The Golden Spike wound up at the museum at Stanford Univer-

▼ *One of America's most treasured photographic icons is this image by Andrew J. Russell, exposed upon a glass plate negative shortly after the Golden Spike ceremony on May 10, 1869. Russell arranged to have the locomotive engineers from each railroad, Mr. Booth of the Central Pacific and Mr. Bradford of the Union Pacific, pose upon their respective engines—the "Jupiter" and No. 119—with champagne bottles in their hands, while on the ground he placed the two chief civil engineers, Samuel J. Montague of the C.P. and General Grenville M. Dodge of the U.P., shaking hands amid a throng of celebrants.*

sity, where it resides today. The laurelwood tie was destroyed in the earthquake and fire in San Francisco in 1906. The silver spike donated by Nevada was given to Leland Stanford and wound up alongside the Golden Spike at the Stanford University museum. Arizona's composite metal spike has been displayed at the Smithsonian Institution and the Union Pacific Museum in Omaha.

The fate of the second gold spike, presented by newspaperman Frederick Marriott, owner of the San Francisco *News-Letter*, is unknown. The newspaper's offices were destroyed in the 1906 earthquake and fire, however, and the gold spike may well have been lost at that time.

▲ *This colorful poster was commissioned by the Union Pacific to celebrate the completion of the Pacific Railroad.*

# RAILS TO...

# *The Golden Gate*

*THEY HAD AN EYE TOWARD SAN FRANCISCO AND THE NEED TO BRIDGE THE 90-MILE DISTANCE BETWEEN THE CAPITAL AND THE PREMIER CITY OF THE WEST.*

■ *"Riders complained that the Western Pacific's route to San Francisco was too roundabout, and this probably influenced the Big Four's decision to gain control of the Cal-P in 1871."*

At the same time that the Big Four were struggling to complete the link between Sacramento and Omaha, they also had an eye toward San Francisco and the contractual need to bridge the 90-mile distance between the California state capital and the premier city of the West.

Two existing railroads then provided service between Sacramento and San Francisco: the California Pacific and the Western Pacific (no relation to the large Western Pacific "Feather River Route" of later years).

The Western Pacific Railroad was built by a construction company wholly owned by the Central Pacific. It provided service from Sacramento to Oakland and San Jose via Niles, Tracy and Stockton. Construction on the railroad began in January, 1865 and was completed at the end of 1869.

The California Pacific, or Cal-P as it was known, was incorporated in 1865 and offered competing service to the Bay Area. Cal-P trains traveled from Sacramento to Vallejo, where their cargo was transferred to San Francisco Bay Area-bound ferries. In addition, the company also ran a branch line from Davis to Marysville.

Initial Central Pacific operation of transcontinental passenger trains between Sacramento and Oakland, on the eastern side of San Francisco Bay, began on November 8, 1869–thereby satisfying the contractual obligations of the Pacific Railroad Act. Passengers on the transcontinental trains soon began complaining, however, that the Western Pacific's route to San Francisco was too roundabout, and this probably influenced the Big Four's decision to gain control of the Cal-P in 1871. After assuming ownership, the Big Four decided that the ferry ride from Vallejo to the Bay

▶ *The first railroad station in Oakland, California, is shown in 1869.*

▼ *A Western Pacific Railroad train waits for a ferry at the Oakland pier in December, 1869.*

■ *"The Western Pacific Railroad was built by a construction company wholly owned by the Central Pacific. It provided service from Sacramento to Oakland and San Jose via Niles, Tracy and Stockton."*

xciv SAN FRANCISCO DIRECTORY.

**CENTRAL PACIFIC RAILROAD.**

**Quick Time and Cheap Fares**
FROM
CHINA AND JAPAN TO NEW YORK AND LIVERPOOL.

THE GREAT OVERLAND ROUTE
VIA
**Central Pacific Railroad**

Is now in complete running order from
SAN FRANCISCO TO THE ATLANTIC SEABOARD.

Through Express Trains leave San Francisco Daily,
Making prompt connections with the several Railway Lines in the Eastern States for all the Cities of the UNITED STATES AND CANADAS, and connecting at New York with the several steamer lines to
**England, France and all European Ports.**

SILVER PALACE SLEEPING COACHES,
Second to none in the world, are run daily from San Francisco to New York and intermediate points. These Drawing Room Cars by day, and Sleeping Cars by night, are unexcelled for comfort and convenience to the passenger while en route—combining the elegance of a private parlor and all accommodations pertaining to a well-furnished chamber, with comfortable couches, clean bedding, etc. A competent Porter accompanies each Car to attend to the wants of our patrons.

**GREAT REDUCTION IN THROUGH FARES.**
Children not over Twelve (12) years of age, HALF FARE. Under Five (5) years of age, FREE. 100 pounds of Baggage per Adult Passenger, FREE. 50 pounds of Baggage, per child between 5 and 12, FREE.

Through Ticket Office, 422 CALIFORNIA ST., San Francisco.

Through Freights between San Francisco and New York, and other Eastern Cities, contracted through at low rates. Mark Goods "CARE C. P. R. R." ☞ *Money saved by purchasing Tickets at the Company's Offices.*

**T. H. GOODMAN,** Gen'l Freight and Passenger Agent.
**A. N. TOWNE,** General Superintendent.

took too long, so by 1879 they had completed a rail link between Martinez and Oakland.

After that trains from Sacramento rode the tracks to Benicia, where they were transported across the Carquinez Straits on ferries large enough to carry an entire passenger train. In 1930 the Benicia Bridge was built, eliminating the need for the ferries to Port Costa.

◀ *A Central Pacific Railroad train draws the attention of onlookers on the Oakland pier.*

# SIGN OF THE TIMES: *Immigrant Trains*

*England, Germany, and Scandinavia were among the areas where rail companies maintained full-time recruitment operations, rounding up as many immigrants as possible.*

■ *"The immigrants were usually separated by sex. Women rode in one car and men in another, except when large families traveled together. Sleeping was accomplished by curling up on a wooden bench."*

▲ *Passengers on a Central Pacific train at Cape Horn, California enjoy the view from the mountain observation car.*

The completion of rail routes to the West opened a new era of immigration for the United States as railroad companies such as the Central Pacific and Union Pacific undertook wholesale efforts to import buyers for the millions of acres of land they now owned.

The rail companies had taken title to the land as part of their agreements with the federal government, but the real estate was relatively worthless without buyers.

England, Germany, and Scandinavia were among the areas where U.S. rail companies maintained full-time recruitment operations, paying for newspaper advertising and posters and the salary of an agent whose job it was to round up as many immigrants as possible. The agents often found their best targets among groups who were experiencing political or religious persecution. That's how a large contingent of Mennonite wheat farmers came to Kansas from Czarist Russia, for instance. Fifteen thousand Mennonites ultimately settled in Kansas, bringing with them the knowledge of wheat and dairy farming that would mold the economy of that breadbasket state.

Lured by promises of prosperity and comfort, the immigrants found by the time they arrived in New York that all wasn't as wonderful as had been advertised by the agents. The accommodations on the cross-country trains were certainly vastly different from those experienced by the well-heeled passengers who could afford elegant Pullman Palace cars.

The Union Pacific and other railroads provided very old and spartan coaches for the immigrants. Many of these cars had been converted from obsolete day-coaches. There were no cushions on the hard wood benches and no springs to soften the ride.

The immigrants were usually separated by sex. Women rode in one car and men in another, ex-

◄ *Accommodations on the coaches that immigrants rode were adequate for short trips but uncomfortable for a journey of a week's duration.*

◄ *Transcontinental travel became romanticized after the completion of the Pacific Railroad, but for those who made the long trip on immigrant trains conditions were anything but plush.*

◄ *The passengers aboard a Central Pacific immigrant train take a moment to pose at Mill City, Nevada.*

cept when large families traveled together. Sleeping was accomplished by curling up on a wooden bench, perhaps on a straw-filled pad that had been purchased for a high price from a porter.

# *Elegance Rides the Rails*

*WRITERS, TYCOONS, THEATRE PEOPLE, THE TASTEMAKERS OF THE DAY, ALL HAD TO HAVE THE EXPERIENCE OF RIDING COAST-TO-COAST ON THE NEW TRANSCONTINENTAL LINE.*

■ *"Travel time between New York and San Francisco was seven days. This included about four changes of train which, in themselves, added considerably to the trip."*

▲ *A group of well-heeled travelers detrains to savor the view at Cape Horn in the Sierra Nevada mountains during the 1870s.*

The mystique of elegant travel by train across the West was at its height in the last 25 years of the 1800s. Writers, tycoons, theater people—the tastemakers of the day—all had to have the experience of riding coast-to-coast on the new transcontinental line.

Rudyard Kipling, Frank and Mirian Leslie, Oscar Wilde, Bret Harte, Helen Hunt Jackson, and a handful of U.S. Presidents were among the passengers on westbound trains whose travels whetted the public's appetite for transcontinental travel.

George Pullman provided the cars that would make the well-to-do feel at home on the rails. For a while Webster Wagner produced cars that competed in comfort and accommodations, but Pullman bought out Wagner to corner the market.

Travel time between New York and San Francisco was seven days. This included about four changes of train which, in themselves, added considerably to the trip. Only one experiment is recorded in which a passenger train made the trip as an express coast to coast: Jarrett & Palmer's Transcontinental Express, organized for the United States centennial of 1876 by two theatrical promoters.

The organizers managed to talk the railroads along the way into clearing the tracks so the Lightning Train, as it was called, could make its record-breaking run. Passengers paid $500 per ticket to ride the train, which made the trip from coast to coast in 83 hours.

Big crowds turned out along the way to cheer the Lightning Train on, but after the feat was accomplished, railroad owners showed little interest in running regular express service coast to coast. Even 100 years later the best time an Amtrak passenger could expect to make, if all trains were on time, was about seventy-four hours.

Accommodations in the Pullman sleeper coaches were relatively comfortable, although many passengers complained that dressing and undressing was difficult in the horizontal sleeping compartments. The lack of privacy and waiting lines at the washstand each morning also drew criticism.

PALACE-CAR LIFE ON THE PACIFIC RAILROAD.

◀ *An idealization of travel upon the transcontinental railway as published in a periodical in the early 1870s. At this time in America's history only the wealthiest citizens could afford this standard of travel.*

■ *"Accommodations in the Pullman sleeper coaches were relatively comfortable, although many passengers complained that dressing and undressing was difficult in the horizontal sleeping compartments."*

▲ *The Pullman Palace drawing room and sleeping car "Woodstock" epitomized stylish travel after the completion of the transcontinental railroad.*

◀ *Not all of Central Pacific's or Union Pacific's passengers rode inside the cars. As depicted in Leslie's Weekly of February 2, 1878, tramps and drifters attempted to ride the transcontinental trains in ways discouraged by management.*

# *Locomotives & Shops*

*THE FIRST LOCOMOTIVES THAT THE CENTRAL PACIFIC BOUGHT HAD TO BE SHIPPED FROM THE EAST COAST AROUND CAPE HORN TO SAN FRANCISCO, A JOURNEY OF OVER 10,000 MILES.*

■ *"Collis Huntington and his partners soon began buying up rolling stock wherever they could get it at a good price on the West Coast, to save the cost of shipping it around the Horn."*

The first locomotives that the Central Pacific bought had to be shipped from the East Coast around Cape Horn to San Francisco, a journey of over 10,000 miles. While the Union Pacific bestowed only numbers on its engines for identification purposes, the Central Pacific for a time gave names to its locomotives as well.

The CP's first four locomotives were the *Governor Stanford*, *Pacific*, *C.P. Huntington*, and *T.D. Judah*, Numbers 1, 2, 3, and 4, respectively.

The C.P. Huntington later became Southern Pacific engine No. 1 when the Big Four consolidated their holdings. The little engine was almost scrapped but eventually wound up being restored and currently is a premier showpiece of the California State Railroad Museum in Sacramento. The *Huntington* is only 29.5 feet long, with a 4-2-4 wheel layout. Also on display at the museum is the *Governor Stanford*.

▲*C.P. No. 166—the third locomotive to bear that number—was built in the company's Sacramento Shops in November, 1886.*

Collis Huntington and his partners soon began buying up rolling stock wherever they could get it at a good price on the West Coast, to save the cost of shipping it around the Horn. In 1864, in a transaction that required no cash, they bought half the rolling stock of the California Central Railroad for $105,000 in discounted Central Pacific stocks and bonds. Included were four locomotives and four passenger cars, three box cars, and 23 flat cars. All had to be regauged to run on the Central Pacific tracks.

The Big Four ultimately decided they needed their own facility for manufacturing locomotives. Within three years of completion of the transcontinental line, the Central Pacific's Sacramento Shops were turning out complete locomotives. The earliest engines built in Sacramento were of the 4-4-0 type, being 52 feet long and weighing 33 tons.

In the ensuing 65 years the venerable Sacramento Shops turned out over 200 locomotives, not ceasing production until 1937, when it switched to strictly a maintenance function. Many of the original shop buildings exist today, and plans are being prepared to preserve them for the use and enjoyment of future generations.

◀ *Car shop No. 3 at the Central Pacific's Sacramento Shops complex produced numerous passenger and freight cars.*

■ *"Many of the original shop buildings exist today, and plans are being prepared to preserve them for the use and enjoyment of future generations."*

◀ *The newly-erected Central Pacific shops in Sacramento, circa 1869.*

▼ *Site of the future Central Pacific shops in Sacramento in the late 1860s, after heavy rains caused the overflowing of the Sacramento River.*

◀ *The Central Pacific's car and blacksmith shops at Sacramento in 1870.*

▲ *C.P. locomotive No. 25 at Terrace, Utah, in 1870. Note the ornate iron work that supported the massive headlight.*

# THE RAILROAD AND *Native Americans*

*The Paiutes interacted in a friendly if aloof fashion with the Chinese workers, telling new arrivals that there were monstrous snakes in the desert that could devour a man whole.*

■ *"After the attack on the commissioners, the federal government provided more cavalry to protect the railroad crews."*

The Central Pacific and the Union Pacific had some problems in common, and some problems that were uniquely their own. The presence along the construction route of Native Americans, or Indians as they were called, presented very different situations for the two railroads.

The Central Pacific experienced virtually no violent outbreaks with the Paiutes and Shoshones whom they encounted after descending the eastern side of the Sierra. The railroad even went so far as to execute its own treaty with the Paiutes, an Apache subtribe. By and large, the Central Pacific treated the Indians with great respect, providing them with free passes to ride the trains and putting a number of them on the payroll.

The Paiutes interacted in a friendly if somewhat aloof fashion with the CP's Chinese workers, telling new arrivals by sign language that there were monstrous snakes in the desert that could devour a man whole. Some of the superstitious Chinese believed the natives and fled.

The Union Pacific workers, in contrast, maintained a substantial arsenal to defend themselves against their region's Indians. In the spring and summer of 1867, the crews worked in fear of attacks by Cheyenne and Arapahoe warriors. There were a string of attacks including one against a survey party that resulted in the death of a surveyor's assistant and a soldier.

Sioux warriors killed and scalped five men in a section gang 200 miles west of Omaha, and four more workers died in two subsequent attacks. In May three government commissioners inspecting the line fell prey to the Indians. A party of warriors swept through the camp while the commissioners were eating and stole their horses and mules.

After the attack on the commissioners, the federal government provided more cavalry to protect the railroad crews. Unfortunately, this didn't prevent survey chief Percy Browne from being fatally shot by Sioux warriors at the Continental Divide in July.

▼ *A group of Native Americans poses for A.A. Hart's camera in front of a Central Pacific locomotive. The Central Pacific had little trouble with indigenous populations, in contrast to the hostility encountered by the Union Pacific.*

■ *"After the attack on the commissioners, the federal government provided more cavalry to protect the railroad crews."*

◀ *A band of Ute warriors poses on horseback for A.J. Russell's camera. More hostile tribes launched attacks against U.P. crews as the railroad built across the Great Plains.*

# *Images of the Railway*

*Images of the transcontinental railway have captured the imagination of generations since the road's construction.*

■ *Central Pacific locomotive No. 108 "Stager" at Elko, Nevada, on February 8, 1869, shortly after rails reached this location.*

▶ *Photographer Alfred A. Hart captured a Central Pacific passenger train as it rounded Cape Horn in the early 1870s.*

▼ *Central Pacific Railroad Co. shipping order dated May 26, 1879, for the transportation of one box and one sack of vegetables from Quang Sing of Sacramento to Sun Chung Kee & Co. of Carson City, Nevada.*

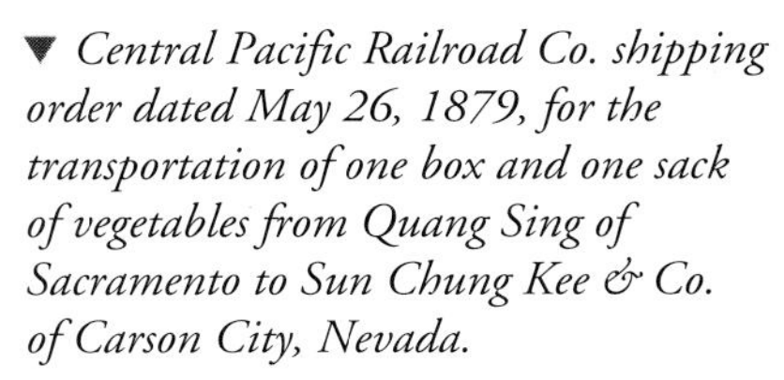

Duplicate.] **Central Pacific Railroad Co.**

No. ____ Sacramento May 26 1879.

**Received of** SUN CHUNG KEE & CO.

by the Central Pacific Railroad Company, the following property, in apparent good order (except as noted) marked and consigned as in the margin, which they agree to deliver with as reasonable dispatch as their general business will permit, subject to the CONDITIONS mentioned below, in like good order (the dangers incident to Railroad Transportation, loss or damage by fire while at Depots or Stations, loss or damage of combustible articles by fire while in transit, and unavoidable accidents excepted) at

Reno

Station, upon the payment of charges. The Company further agree to forward the property to the place of destination as per margin, but are not to be held liable on account thereof after the same shall be delivered as above. The Company, however, guarantee the Through Rate of Freight as designated below.

**CONDITIONS.**—The Company do not agree to carry the property by any particular train nor in time for any particular market.

Oils, and all other fluids at owner's risk of leakage.

Liquids in glass or earthen, drugs and medicines in boxes, glass and glassware in boxes, looking glasses, marble, stoves, stove plates and light castings, earthen or queensware at owner's risk of breakage.

Agricultural implements, cabinet ware and furniture not boxed, carriages, at owner's risk of breakage or damage by chafing.

Oysters, poultry, dressed hogs, fresh meats and provisions of all kinds, trees, shrubbery, fruits, and all perishable property, at owner's risk of frost and decay.

It is a part of this agreement that all other carriers transporting the property herein receipted for, as a part of the through line, shall be entitled to the benefit of all the exceptions and conditions above mentioned, and if a carrier by water he is to be entitled to the further benefit of exception from loss or damage arising from collision, and all other dangers incident to lake and river navigation.

| MARKS AND CONSIGNEES | ARTICLES | WEIGHT |
|---|---|---|
| Quang Sing Quen Carson City | 1 Box Vegt | 64 |
| | 1 Sk " | 50 |

Rate ____ Per ____

From ____

To ____ Agent.

◀ *Stereoscopic photo cards of the original Secrettown Trestle, produced as part of Watkins' Pacific Railroad series. The top view depicts the trestle as viewed from the east, while the lower card shows the trestle from the west.*

▲ *Looking east at Truckee, California, 119.5 miles east of Sacramento, circa 1868.*

◀ *The first Central Pacific construction train to pass through Palisades, Nevada.*

# THE TRANSCONTINENTAL:

# *In Later Years*

*THEY ACQUIRED LINES AND BUILT NEW ONES, CONSOLIDATING MOST OF THEIR HOLDINGS UNDER THE SOUTHERN PACIFIC UMBRELLA.*

■ *"The Big Four became fabulously wealthy as a result of their involvement with the railroad. Collis Huntington ultimately fulfilled his stated dream of being able to ride from coast to coast on rails that he owned."*

After completion of the transcontinental line, the Big Four set their sights north, south, and east. They acquired existing lines and built new ones, consolidating most of their holdings under the Southern Pacific umbrella.

The company first stretched southward in California, through the San Joaquin Valley, to Los Angeles. By 1881 the company was pushing east from Los Angeles, into Arizona and on to El Paso, Texas. The lines continued to stretch east into Texas and Louisiana, and also northward into Oregon.

The Southern Pacific system eventually resembled a giant crescent stretching from Portland to New Orleans, in addition to the segment from Ogden to Oakland.

▲ *Two of the cab-forward locomotives that Southern Pacific designed and had built for the trans-Sierra run are shown here east of Emigrant Gap in June, 1950.*

The Big Four became fabulously wealthy as a result of their involvement with the railroad. Collis Huntington in particular expanded his interest in railroads, acquiring routes or shares in companies in the East and Southeast, enabling him to ultimately fulfill his stated dream of being able to ride from coast to coast on rails that he owned.

The Union Pacific, however, experienced numerous legal and public relations debacles after completion of the transcontinental line. Thomas Durant was forced off the company's board in the spring of 1869 after clashing repeatedly with President Oliver Ames over business philosophy.

Durant had always believed that stock manipulations and construction of the railroad were the best ways to generate money. Ames believed in the more long-term approach of selling company property to homesteaders along the right-of-way as a means to generate financial security for the company. It was Durant's management legacy that was destined to live on, however. A congressional committee in 1872 investigated Credit Mobilier, the Union Pacific's holding company, and the manner in which Credit

◀ *Two Southern Pacific Company steam locomotives, Nos. 2631 and 2902, stop for servicing and water at Blue Canyon in the early 1900s.*
▼ *Modern day photo of Southern Pacific diesel freight train just west of Cisco, California.*

▼ *Early Central Pacific and Union Pacific steam engines lined up at the Ogden, Utah, yards for this photo in the late 1800s.*

Mobilier stock was distributed to members of congress and Union Pacific stockholders. A major scandal erupted as a result of this investigation, forcing many prominent people to lose their fortunes and the Union Pacific into bankruptcy.

▲ *By 1889, when this photo was taken, Colfax, California, had become a vibrant railroad town.*

# THE TRANSCONTINENTAL:
# *Riding the Rails Today*

*IT'S STILL POSSIBLE TO RIDE MUCH OF THE ORIGINAL TRANSCONTINENTAL RAILROAD ON AMTRAK.*

■ *"The transcontinental rail traveler rides the Zephyr from Fort Morgan to Denver, through northern Colorado and southern Utah until joining the route of the original transcontinental railway at Elko, Nevada."*

Today, more than 125 years after the first passengers rode from Omaha to Sacramento on the nation's first transcontinental railway, it is possible to ride passenger trains over much of the original route.

In Omaha, a modern passenger climbs aboard Amtrak's California Zephyr for the trip west. Before Amtrak, the California Zephyr was a venerable transcontinental streamliner jointly operated by the Chicago, Burlington & Quincy, Denver & Rio Grande Western, and Western Pacific railroads; today it ranks as one of Amtrak's most popular long-distance trains.

▶*Amtrak's "California Zephyr" westbound near snow shed 10 in California's beautiful Sierra Nevada mountain range.*

West of Omaha, the Zephyr follows the Burlington Northern to Denver. At Denver, the traveler has two options: stay on the Zephyr for a trip through the Rockies; or, ride part of the original transcontinental route by switching to Amtrak's Pioneer. This train runs north to Cheyenne, and then crosses Wyoming on Union Pacific's historic mainline.

At Ogden, Utah, the Pioneer turns toward Seattle, but an Amtrak Thruway Bus reconnects with the California Zephyr in Salt Lake City. The Zephyr rejoins the original transcontinental route at Elko, Nevada. The train then proceeds past stations evoking images of late Nineteenth Century rail travel—Winnemucca, Sparks, and Reno, Nevada, and Truckee and Roseville, California—before the stop in Sacramento.

The trackage between Sacramento and Winnemucca, Nevada, still uses a much of the original Central Pacific alignment . Major rebuilding of the Sierra trackage occurred in the early 1900s when the Southern Pacific attempted to increase capacity over the line. A second track was added to portions of the route, but recent financial conditions have led to the removal by Southern Pacific of several miles of the original track.

◀ *An Amtrak passenger train makes its way along the track at Alta, California—April 5, 1987.*

■ *"The section of track between Sacramento and Winnemucca, Nevada, still uses a great deal of the original alignment and grades of the Central Pacific Railroad. Major rebuilding and realigning of the Sierra trackage occurred in the early 1900s ."*

◀ *Eastbound Amtrak train at Cape Horn.*

# *Promontory Recreated*

*It's still possible to ride much of the original transcontinental railroad on Amtrak.*

▶ *The two locomotive reproductions draw crowds daily at the Golden Spike National Historic Site.*

▲ *An explanation of A.J. Russell's famous photo is in the foreground as a re-enactment of the Golden Spike ceremony takes place in the background.*

The National Park Service acknowledges the importance that Promontory Summit, Utah, played in the history of the United States by operating the Golden Spike National Historic Site.

The park is located 32 miles west of Brigham City, Utah. Among the attractions are the Visitor Center, steam locomotives, trackside talks, a self-guided auto and walking tour of the original roadbed,

▶ *Locomotives No. 60 "Jupiter" and No. 119 are the big attractions at Golden Spike National Historic Site.*

*◀ The whistle blows on one of the replica locomotives at Golden Spike National Historic Site*

and a variety of special events.

The Visitor Center is open daily except on Thanksgiving, Christmas and New Year's Day. Slide programs, films, and museum exhibits explain the significance of the nation's first transcontinental railroad. There is also a bookstore at the Visitor Center.

Perhaps the biggest attractions at the historic site are the replicas of the two steam locomotives that met at the Golden Spike Ceremony—the "Jupiter" and "119." The two engines are on display daily from May to October, with steam demonstrations on their arrival and departure from the sheds.

The Golden Spike National Historic Site also holds an annual observance of the Golden Spike Ceremony on May 10, including re-enactments by members of the Golden Spike Association.

The park is located in the stark hills of northern Utah, a half-hour drive from the nearest lodgings. The makeshift community that once existed here is long gone, and visitors get a realistic feel for conditions that faced the builders of the transcontinental railway.

The replica locomotives—No. 60 "Jupiter" and No. 119—were constructed by O'Connor Engineering Laboratories of Costa Mesa, California during the period 1975-79. They are copies of the two locomotives that met at Promontory Summit on May 10, 1869.

■ *"Perhaps the biggest attractions at the historic site are the replicas of the two steam locomotives that met at the Golden Spike Ceremony —the "Jupiter" and "119."*

*◀ Locomotive No. 119 is a colorful reminder of the historic events of May 10, 1869.*

## BIBLIOGRAPHY


Athearn, Robert G. *Union Pacific Country.* New York, N.Y., Rand McNally, 1971.

Brown, Dee. *Hear That Lonesome Whistle Blow.* New York, N.Y., Holt, Rinehart and Winston, 1977.

Frey, Robert L., ed. *Railroads in the Nineteenth Century.* New York, Facts On File, 1988

Howard, Robert West. *The Great Iron Trail.* New York, Bonanza Books, 1962.

Klein, Maury. *Union Pacific: The Birth of a Railroad.* New York, Doubleday & Co., 1987.

Lewis, Oscar. *The Big Four.* Sausalito, Calif., Comstock Editions, 1971.

Williams, John Hoyt. *A Great and Shining Road.* New York, Times Books, 1988.

Yenne, Bill. *The History of the Southern Pacific.* New York, Bonanza Books, 1988.


## PHOTO CREDITS

Dick Dorn ........ Page 44
Guy L. Dunscomb ........ Page 31R, 41T
Golden Spike National Historic Site ........ Page 20T, 46B, 47LB
A.A. Hart ........ Page 8L, 9 all, 10, 11 all, 16 all, 17 all, 20L, 21 all, 39, 40 all, 41LB, 41 LR
Clint Nestell ........ Page 3B, 43LM, 45 all
A.J. Russell ........ Page 12 all, 13 all, 26, 28-29, 37LM
Richard Steinheimer ........ Page 3T, 46T, 47T, 47LR
Union Pacific Museum ........ Page 6, 7 all, 14, 15, 27B
Utah Historical Society ........ Page 22, 23
Wilbur C. Whittaker ........ Page 42
Kyle Wyatt ........ Page 33T

All uncredited photos and illustrations from the collection of Jeffrey Moreau.

Map on pages 24-25 by Shirley Burman.

## ABOUT THE AUTHORS

**Jeffrey Moreau** is a lifelong rail enthusiast and has been employed in the transportation industry for almost his entire career. A former associate editor of Interurbans publications, Moreau has, on his own, published seven books on the subject of Western railroading. At present, Jeffrey Moreau is co-authoring, with David G. Stanley, a definitive history of the Central California Traction Company.

**Raymond Cushing** is a freelance writer who began his career in 1972 as a reporter for the *Stamford* (Conn.) *Advocate.* His articles and photographs have appeared in *Texas Monthly*, the *Dallas Morning News*, and numerous trade publications. Cushing co-authored the book *Fire & Gold: The San Francisco Story*, and is currently at work on a biography of Theodore Judah.